Contents

Foreword   2

History   2

The game of golf   3

Etiquette   4

The club   4

The ball   6

Preparing to hit the
    ball   6

    The stance   6
    Address   7
    Ball placement   7
    The grip   8

Making the stroke   9

Putting   10

Keeping the score   11

Rules of the game   12

Etiquette   25

Definitions   26

Index   inside back cover

GW00601172

Photograph acknowledgements
Action-Plus Photographic (cover, pp. 1, 3, 13, 14, 26, 29, 32); Peter Dazeley (pp. 1, 27, 31).

1

Foreword

The Professional Golfers' Association was founded in 1901 to promote interest in the game of golf and to protect and advance the mutual and trade interests of its members. The P.G.A is the oldest such association in the world and is responsible, together with the P.G.A European Tour, for promoting professional tournaments run under its auspices in Europe.

It is most advantageous for any beginner to the game to seek advice from a golf professional who is a member of the P.G.A. He will advise on correct equipment and give tuition on the basic fundamentals of the game which are described in this book. The book is essentially a guide to the game and is not meant to be a complete reference.

The official Rules of Golf are governed by the Royal and Ancient Golf Club of St. Andrews. This book is not meant to be a substitute for the official publication but should be read in conjunction with it. The Rules governing situations described in this book are shown in brackets at the end of each section. The Rules of Golf are published by Royal Insurance and are available free of charge from most golf clubs or by post from Royal Insurance (UK) Ltd, PO Box 144, New Hall Place, Liverpool L69 3EN.

Irrespective of the degree of playing ability actually attained, golf is a pastime which can be enjoyed by young and old alike, and I have pleasure in recommending this book to all who wish to know the game of golf.

John Lindsey
Executive director, Professional Golfers' Association

Note Throughout the book players are referred to individually as 'he'. This should of course be taken to mean 'he or she' where appropriate.

History

The origins of the game of golf have been the subject of much research for many years and still arouse controversy.

It is thought that the game began in Scotland, although several landscapes painted by Dutch and Flemish artists suggest that golf was played in Holland before it was known in Scotland.

The first mention of the game in official records was during the Scottish Parliaments of 1457–1491, when golf was prohibited because its popularity interfered with the practice of archery, to the consequent detriment of the national defence in the wars against England; by the reign of James II, golf had become a national pastime in Scotland.

The Honourable Company of Edinburgh Golfers situated at Muirfield formed the first set of Rules of the game, and these were adopted by the Society of St. Andrews Golfers which was formed in 1754.

In 1834 King William IV approved

The game of golf

the change of name of the Society to the Royal and Ancient Golf Club of St. Andrews, which is now responsible for the government of the game, the interpretation of the Rules and the control of the Open Championship.

The following organisations are responsible for the control of amateur golf in their respective areas: the English Golf Union (founded 1924), the Golfing Union of Ireland (founded 1891), the Scottish Golf Union (founded 1920) and the Welsh Golfing Union (founded 1895).

With the spread of the game overseas many organisations have been formed, the most significant being the United States Golf Association (U.S.G.A.) founded in 1894, which is responsible for governing all aspects of the game in America and has close contact with the Royal and Ancient Golf Club to maintain uniformity in the administration of the game.

Playing the ball from the teeing ▶ ground

'The Game of Golf consists in playing a ball from the teeing ground into the hole by successive strokes in accordance with the Rules.' (*Rule 1*)

A full-sized course consists of 18 holes: usually four 'short' holes, which measure up to 250 yards (229 m) from tee to green and can be covered by one full stroke; and 14 longer holes, from 250 to 500 yards (229 to 457 m) or more in length, and requiring two or three full strokes from tee to green. One round of the course is the usual length of a match, but in some competitions two or more rounds are played. One round occupies about three hours.

The space between tee and green at the long holes is occupied by mown turf called the 'fairway', and on either side of the fairway are rough grass, trees, bushes, etc. There are also 'hazards' of various kinds, mainly sand bunkers but occasionally streams, ditches, and ponds. The green is a closely mown surface for putting and the 'hole' is sunk in the green and marked with a flag.

3

Etiquette

In addition to the rules, the game also has a code of etiquette, which should be observed by all golfers and studied with particular care by beginners. Adherence to these rules of behaviour helps to make the game more enjoyable for everyone. The rules of etiquette are quoted in full on page 25–6, but can be summarised as follows:

1 Do not move, talk, stand close to or directly behind the ball or the hole when a player is making a stroke.

2 Do not play until the match in front is out of range, but do not unnecessarily delay play.

3 If overtaken by a following match while searching for a ball, or because of your own slow play, signal to the over-taking players to pass, and then wait until they have gone out of range before continuing play.

4 Smooth over holes and footmarks made in bunker sand before leaving it, and see that all turf cut by the club-head is replaced and pressed down.

5 Avoid damage to greens by clubs, feet or flagstick, and repair marks made by the ball when landing. After placing the flagstick, walk off quickly once the result of the hole is determined, without re-trying putts, so that the way is clear for following players.

6 Make sure that no one is in a position to sustain injury from your stroke or practice swing.

The club

Two rules prohibit the use of any club or ball which does not conform to clearly-defined specifications and fundamental principles of design. Clubs must have all the various parts fixed and not capable of adjustment. Concave faces are banned, also those having markings which do not satisfy the current requirements or are modified for the

Fig. 1 Some club-heads now illegal ▼

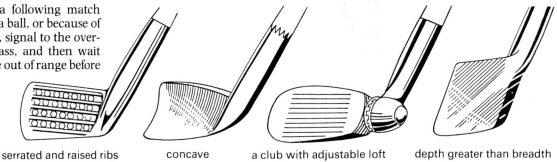

serrated and raised ribs   concave   a club with adjustable loft   depth greater than breadth

purpose of unduly influencing the movement of the ball.

The grip on the shaft may not have a channel or furrow or be moulded to the hands, and the shaft itself must be fixed to the heel of the club-head, except in the case of a putter. The shaft of a putter may be fixed at any point in the head, but must be straight and must diverge from the vertical by at least ten degrees from a point not more than five inches above the sole.

An 'iron' club is one with a head which is usually relatively narrow from face to back, and is usually made of steel. A 'wood' club is one with a head relatively broad from face to back, and is usually made of wood, plastic, or a light metal. (*Rule 4*)

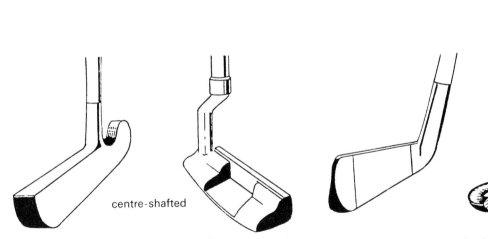

centre-shafted

Fig. 2 Modern examples of putters

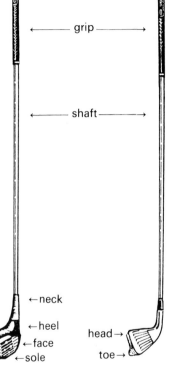

grip

shaft

←neck

←heel

←face

head→

←sole

toe→

Fig. 3 The wood and the iron

5

The ball

The weight of the ball may not be greater than 1.62 ounces (45.9 grammes) and the size not less than 1.68 inches (42.7 mm) in diameter. There is also a velocity standard and only balls on the approved lists of conforming balls of the R. & A. and U.S.G.A. are legal. (*Rule 5*)

Although golf in its earliest and unrecorded days was probably played with odd missiles such as pebbles or lumps of wood, the first ball known to history was the 'featherie' – a leather bag stuffed tightly with feathers and then stitched. This was at best an ill-flying ball with a very short life, particularly in wet weather, but it remained in general use for more than two centuries until the advent of the 'guttie' over a century ago. This was made from gutta-percha, softened and cast in a spherical mould, originally hand-hammered to make it fly straight. Later, moulds with embossed or recessed patterns came into use.

In the late 1890s the Haskell ball, made from strip rubber wound round a core, was produced in America, and first used in Britain in 1902. It soon ousted the guttie, and the rubber-core ball, as it is called, is now made to perfection by up-to-date machinery, and with reasonable care will last for many rounds of golf without losing shape or resilience.

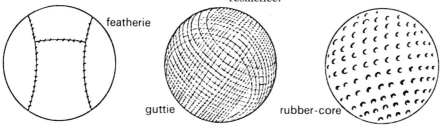

featherie

guttie

rubber-core

Fig. 4 The ball

Preparing to hit the ball

The stance

A player has 'addressed the ball' when he has taken his stance and has also grounded his club (or, in a hazard, has taken his stance).

The stance, or position taken by the feet in preparing for the stroke, varies with the build of the player, his method of swinging and the type of shot being attempted, but generally speaking, the feet are straddled along a line which is parallel to the line of intended flight of the ball.

The width of the stance also varies with players and types of shot, but a good rule is to stand so that the distance between the feet is about equal to the width of the shoulders. As the shots to the green get shorter, so the stance narrows. The whole idea should be to use the minimum width of stance consistent with good balance. Too wide a stance restricts the pivoting of the body. Too narrow a stance makes the body sway, which is disadvantageous.

There are three basic stances: square, open and closed; and the one used depends upon the club chosen and the type of shot to be played.

The square stance is used for most long shots with the woods and long irons. The open stance is used mostly for bad lies, short shots and approach play etc. The closed stance is used when it is necessary to putt, draw or hook on the ball.

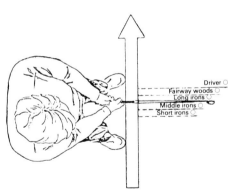

Fig. 5 Square stance, showing ball positions

Address

At the address position, the feet should be approximately as far apart as the width of the player's shoulders, with the weight evenly distributed between the feet; the toes should be pointed outwards very slightly and the knees flexed slightly inwards. The left arm, wrist and club should be virtually in a straight line, with the hands slightly ahead of the club-head. The body should not be too crouched or too upright in position, but just between the two.

If the ball moves after address it must be replaced, and not played as it lays.

Fig. 6 Open stance

Ball placement

When using a driver, the ball is placed opposite the left heel; for fairway woods and long irons just inside the left heel; for middle irons, between the centre of the feet and the left heel, with the feet now getting closer together; and for short irons, midway between the feet which should now be about nine inches apart.

The next thing to consider is the distance from the ball. This depends again on the build of the golfer and the size of club used, but the guiding factor is comfort and relaxation. One should feel comfortably settled down for hitting the

Fig. 7 Closed stance

ball, neither over-reaching for it nor hunched up.

For the driver a good tip is to rest the club-head behind the ball and stand so that the outstretched arm, holding the club, makes a straight line from shoulder to ball, while the body stands erect. Then bend forward to place the right hand on the shaft, and the position is correct.

Another test is to take up a stance and then take away the right hand, dropping the club with the left until it touches the thigh above the left knee. This shows again that the distance is correct.

The grip

Although there are several ways of gripping a club, some of them highly unorthodox, the grip most commonly used is the overlapping or 'Vardon' grip (see fig. 8), so called after its originator Harry Vardon, who won the British Open Championship on a record six occasions between 1896 and 1914.

Commence by placing the left hand on the club: it must be a combination of finger and palm grip. The club must lie across the hands from the middle joint of the first finger, over the base of the middle finger and into the heel of the hand (a).

When the hand is closed, the thumb should be a quarter of the way round the shaft to the right and the tip of the thumb in line with the knuckle of the first finger (b). The 'V' formed between the thumb and the first finger should point between the chin and the right shoulder.

The right hand is a finger grip. To help the two hands to work together the little finger of the right hand overlaps the first finger of the left hand (c).

The grip lies across the middle joint of the other three fingers and the palm of the right hand fits snugly over the left thumb. The 'V' formed between the thumb and forefinger also points to a spot between the chin and the right shoulder (d). There should now be a firm and lively connection of the hands and the club-head.

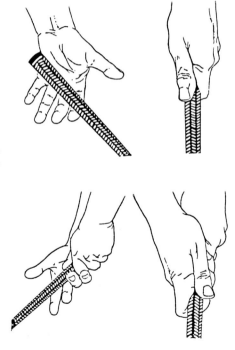

Fig. 8 The Vardon grip

Making the stroke

A 'stroke' is the forward movement of the club made with the intention of fairly striking at and moving the ball.

The mechanics of the golf swing consist in swinging the club backwards and upwards from the address position to a position above and behind the head from which a downward and forward blow can be aimed at the ball. The accompanying sketches should make clear the sequence of movements, but there are certain principles to bear in mind.

The club-head is taken back from the ball by a co-ordinated movement of various parts of the body, which pivots or turns on an axis formed by the spine. The hands lead; while the left heel may leave the ground, the left knee bends inwards and sideways, and the shoulders and hips turn. The head remains still throughout the swing, the chin pointing towards the ball, and when the club-head is half-way up to the top of the swing position the wrists begin to bend or 'cock' (b). At the top of the swing the club shaft should be almost horizontal and the club head pointing at the target (c).

The start of the down-swing is a general 'pull-down' of the left side, hands and arms leading (d), and then the rest of the down-swing is a progressive speeding up of the club-head, which is whipped into the ball in a flail-like manner (e). The whole movement, up and down, should be rhythmic and controlled.

A natural sequel to the down-swing is the 'follow-through', in which the body turns in the direction of flight and the club-head is flung out in the same direction (f) until at the finish of the stroke the trunk is square towards the hole, the hands high, and the club-shaft behind the back (g).

The golf swing is more or less the same for all maximum-length shots, no matter what club is used, but in the case of short pitches or run-up shots when near to the green, the back-swing must be restricted according to the length of the shot. This can only be judged by practice and experience.

Fig. 9 Making the stroke

Putting

Putting is the most precise part of the game and arguably the most important, for strokes can be saved by good putting and wasted by bad putting. The normal average allowance is two putts per green, but a golfer who is putting well usually beats this average.

When the ball lies a fair distance from the hole the stroke is called an 'approach putt', and demands accurate judgement of strength and line. If the green at that part is level, it may be a 'straight putt', but more often the stroke requires a 'borrow' (the ball is then aimed at a point to right or left to allow for the slope).

Then the player must estimate the strength of the putt. If the green slopes down towards the hole, less power will be required than if the putt is uphill. Again, the green might be 'slow' after rain or because the grass has grown, or 'fast' because of hot sunshine or strong wind. This is one area of the game where the Vardon grip is not used and is replaced by a grip with the thumb directly down the handle.

Having summed up the situation to his own satisfaction, the player makes a trial swing to make sure he has the desired stroke well in mind, and then gets his putter blade at right-angles to the intended line and immediately behind the ball. He takes a short or long back-swing, according to the type of stroke, and delivers a firm smooth stroke, keeping the putter blade as far as possible on the line intended.

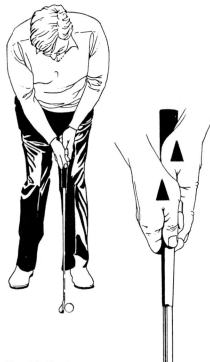

Fig. 10 Putting

Keeping the score

Cards like the specimen shown on this page are used for marking a competitor's score in a Medal, Stableford or Match Play Against Par (Bogey) competition. In Medal play the competitor's full handicap is deducted from his total score. In Stableford competitions it is usual that seven-eighths of the handicap is taken and in Match Play Against Par (Bogey) competitions three-quarters of the handicap is taken. In matches, the player with the higher handicap receives three-quarters of the difference between his handicap and that of his opponent.

Column 1 gives number of the hole.
Column 2 gives length of hole, measured from competition tees.
Column 3 gives the par of the hole.
Column 4 indicates where handicap strokes are taken in Match Play Against Par (Bogey) or Stableford competitions. For example, a player having 12 strokes takes one at the 5th (numbered 12) and one each at all other holes having figures less than 12. A player having only three strokes takes them at the 2nd, 9th and 14th holes.

Column 5 is for the player's score in strokes. This is always given as the gross score, the number of strokes actually played and inserted by the marker. Handicap calculations are made afterwards.

Column 6 shows the results of each hole compared with par. If the player's net score for the hole (after deducting any handicap stroke) is less than the par score he marks '+' indicating a win. If the score is the same the Committee marks '0', indicating a halved hole. If the score is high the Committee marks '–' indicating a loss.

The card shown on this page is marked out for a player going round in 71 net, and finishing one over par in stroke play competition, or finishing all square in a Match Play Against Par (Bogey) competition. The stars indicate those items which are the Committee's responsibility. Both the player and marker *must* sign the card before it is handed in.

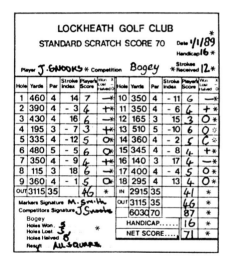

Fig. 11 The score card

Rules of the game

Number of clubs allowed

The player cannot start a round with more than 14 clubs. He may replace any club which becomes unfit for use in the normal course of play by borrowing from any other person playing on the course. The person from whom the club was borrowed may not thereafter use it during the course of his round.

In match play, the penalty for violation of this rule is the loss of a hole for each hole at which the violation occurred, with a maximum of two holes. In stroke play, it is two strokes for each hole at which the violation occurred, with a maximum of four strokes.

A complete 'matched set' of 14 clubs can be obtained, consisting usually of either four woods, nine irons and a putter; or three woods, ten irons and a putter, depending on the individual preference of the player.

The length of a golf club varies from roughly 42 in (107 cm) for a driver to 35 in (89 cm) for a short iron or putter, diminishing at half-inch (1.3 cm) inter-

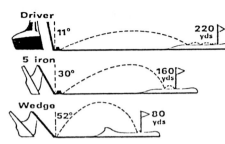

Fig. 12 The loft of a club

vals. As the club diminishes in length, so the club face increases in weight and angle of loft, e.g. the driver at 42 in (107 cm) has an angle of loft on its face of 11°, the five iron at 38 in (97 cm) has an angle of loft on its face of 30°, and the wedge at 36 in (91 cm) has an angle of 52°.

Women's clubs are lighter and slightly shorter than those used by men, and matched sets are 'fitted' to the players, some requiring lighter or shorter clubs, than the standard sizes, or shafts with varying degrees of 'whip'. (*Rule 4–4*)

Waiving the rules

Players must not agree among them-selves to waive a rule, local rule or any penalty incurred. (*Rule 1–3*)

General penalty

Except when otherwise provided for, the penalty for the breach of a rule is the loss of a hole in match play or two strokes in stroke play.

Note This is the usual penalty, but certain minor infringements incur a penalty of one stroke. Generally speaking, disqualification occurs only in the case of deliberate infringement. (*Rules 2–6 and 3–5*)

Types of play

Match play

In match play, a hole is won by the side which holes its ball in the fewest strokes (after deducting any handicap allowance). The hole is halved if each side holes out in the same number of strokes. A match consists of a stipulated round or rounds, and is won by the side which is leading by a number of holes greater than the number remaining to be played. A player can concede his opponent's next stroke, a hole or the match;

this concession may not be declined or withdrawn.

Note Thus, if a side is four up after playing 15 holes, they have won the match by four up and three to play (usually written as 4 & 3). If, after finishing the eighteenth hole, each side has won an equal number, the match is halved. If a decision is essential, as in a knock-out tournament or championship, it is usual for the players to begin the round again, the first to win a hole taking the match. Thus a game can be won at the 19th, the 20th and so on. In playing additional holes, handicap strokes are given and taken at the same holes as in the first round. (*Rule 2*)

Stroke play
The competitor who holes the stipulated round or rounds in the fewest strokes is the winner.

Note In stroke competitions under handicap, the full handicap allowed the player is deducted from his total, and the net score counts. (*Rule 3*)

Practice during play

During the play of a hole, a player must not play any practice stroke. Between the play of two holes a player cannot play a practice stroke from any hazard, but may practice putting or chipping on or near the putting green of the hole last played, any practice putting green or the teeing ground of the next hole to be played in the round. On any day of a stroke competition or play-off, the competitor may not practise on the competition course before a round or play-off. When a competition extends over consecutive days or on different courses, practice on any competition course still to be played between rounds is prohibited.

It is important to note that a practice swing is not a practice stroke, as a stroke is a forward movement of the club with the intention of striking a ball. (*Rule 7*)

Advice and assistance during play

A player may only give advice to, or ask advice from, his partner or either of their caddies. In making a stroke a player must not seek or accept physical assistance or protection from the weather

A player may have the line of play indicated by anyone (except on the putting green, where only the player's partner or caddie may do so), but no one can place a mark or stand to indicate the line of play while the stroke is being played.

Note 'Assistance' or 'protection' includes bending back an obstructing bush or shielding a player from wind or rain. (*Rules 8 and 14–2*)

Only the player's partner or caddie may indicate the line of play

Information as to strokes taken

A player who has incurred a penalty must tell his opponent or marker as soon as possible. The number of strokes a player has taken includes any penalty strokes incurred. A player in match play is entitled at any time during the play of a hole to ask the number of strokes his opponent has taken. If the opponent gives wrong information and fails to correct the mistake before the player has played his next stroke, the opponent loses the hole. (*Rule 9*)

Disputes, decisions and doubts as to rights

In match play where there is a dispute about the rules or the number of strokes taken, a claim must be made before the players strike off from the next teeing ground or (in the case of the last hole of the match) before they leave the putting green. Any later claim based on newly discovered facts cannot be considered unless the player making the claim had been given the wrong information by an opponent. In stroke play no penalty may be imposed after the results are posted or prizes presented, unless the player knowingly returns a score for a hole lower than actually achieved.

If a referee has been appointed by the Committee, his decision is final. In the absence of a referee, the decision of the Committee is final. If the Committee cannot come to a decision, it refers to the Rules of the Golf Committee of the Royal and Ancient Golf Club of St. Andrews, and its decision is final.

If any point in dispute is not covered by the rules or local rules, the decision is made in accordance with fair play and logic, which is referred to in golf as 'equity'.

In stroke play, a competitor who is unsure of his rights or the correct procedure may play out the hole with the original ball and, at the same time, complete the play of the hole with a second ball stating which ball he wishes to score with if that procedure is allowable under the rules. The point is then referred to the committee for adjudication. If a competitor fails to announce in advance his decision to invoke this rule or state in advance the ball with which he wishes to score, the score with the original ball, rather than the higher score, will count. A player need not report the facts to the committee if he scores the same with both balls.

These rules do not apply to match play. (*Rules 2–5, 3–3 and 34*)

Order of play on the tee – 'The honour'

A match begins by each side playing a ball from the first teeing ground in order of the draw or by lot. The side which wins a hole takes 'the honour', i.e. plays first at the next teeing ground. In match play an opponent may recall a ball played out of turn, but in stroke play the stroke must stand. In neither case is there any penalty. (*Rule 10*)

The teeing ground

The teeing ground is the starting place for the hole to be played. It is a rectangular area two club-lengths in depth, the front and sides of which are defined by the outside limits of two markers. A ball is outside the teeing ground when all of it lies outside the area defined above.

Note The teeing ground is not necessarily the whole of the flat space prepared for teeing, but only that part in use for the day. The position of the markers is varied from day to day to avoid undue wear and tear of any one particular area. (*Rule 11*)

◀ Playing from the first teeing ground

Playing outside the teeing ground

If a player in a match, when starting a hole, plays a ball from outside the teeing ground there is no penalty, but his opponent may require him to play the stroke again from within the teeing ground. In stroke play, however, he is penalised two strokes and must play the stroke again from the correct place. Strokes played by a competitor from outside the teeing ground do not count in his score. If a competitor fails to rectify his mistake before making a stroke off the next teeing ground or, in the case

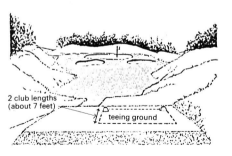

Fig. 13 The teeing ground

of the last hole of the round, before leaving the putting green, he is disqualified.

A player may take his stance outside the teeing ground to play a ball within it. (*Rule 11*)

Ball falling off tee

If a ball, when not in play (that is, when a stroke has not yet been made at it) falls off the tee, or is knocked off by the player in addressing it, it may be re-teed without penalty. (*Rule 11-2*)

Order of play in threesome and foursome

In a foursome (two players playing one ball against a similar pair) the partners strike off alternately from the teeing grounds (*A* drives at the first hole and *B* at the second, etc.), and thereafter the partners strike alternately during the play of each hole.

In match play, if a player tees off when his partner should have done, his side loses the hole. The penalty in stroke play is two strokes, or disqualification if the stroke is not rectified by replaying the stroke in the correct order. (*Rule 29*)

Ball played as it lies

The ball should be played as it lies at all times except where the rules or local rules provide otherwise. (*Rule 13–1*)

Improving lie or stance and influencing ball

Irregularities of surface which could affect a player's lie may not be removed or pressed down by the player, his partner or either of their caddies except: as may occur in fairly taking his stance; in making the stroke or the backward movement of his club for the stroke; when teeing a ball; or repairing damage to the putting green.

If a ball lies in long grass, rushes, bushes, whins, heather or the like, only so much can be touched as will enable the player to find and identify his ball: nothing may be done which can in any way improve its lie.

A player may not improve, or allow to be improved, his line of play, the position or lie of his ball or the area of his intended swing, by bending, moving or breaking anything fixed or growing (except in taking a fair stance to address the ball, and in making the stroke). (*Rules 13–2 and 12–1*)

Loose impediments

A loose impediment may be removed without penalty except when both the impediment and the ball lie in or touch a hazard. When a ball is moving, a loose impediment on the line of play cannot be removed. (*Rule 23*)

The term 'loose impediments' includes natural objects not fixed or growing and not sticking to the ball, e.g. stones not solidly embedded, leaves, twigs, branches and the like, dung, worms and insects and casts or heaps made by them.

Snow and ice are either casual water or loose impediments, at the option of the player. Dew, however, is not a loose impediment.

Sand and loose soil are loose impediments on the putting green, but not elsewhere on the course. (See *Definitions.*)

Striking at the ball

The ball should be firmly struck with the head of the club, and must not be pushed, scraped or spooned (see fig. 14).

If a player, when making a stroke, strikes the ball more than once he counts the stroke and adds a penalty stroke – making two strokes in all. (*Rule 14*)

Fig. 14 Scooping the ball is illegal

Ball farther from the hole played first

When the balls are in play, the ball farthest from the hole must be played first. In match play, if a player plays when his opponent should have done so, the opponent may immediately require the player to replay the stroke. In stroke play no penalty is incurred, and the ball should be played as it lies. (*Rule 10*)

Playing a wrong ball or playing from a wrong place

A player must hole out with the ball driven from the teeing ground unless he has substituted his ball with another.

Note Generally there is a penalty for playing the wrong ball of two strokes in stroke play or loss of hole in match play. However, if a player in a stroke competition holes out with the wrong ball he is disqualified, unless he rectifies his mistake by finding and holing out with his own ball from the place where the mistake occurred, and provided he has not played a stroke from the next teeing ground. In match play if each side plays the other side's ball and it cannot be settled which side first committed the error, the hole shall be played out with the balls thus exchanged. (*Rule 15*)

Lifting, dropping, placing, identifying or cleaning ball

Through the green or in a hazard, when a ball is lifted under a rule or local rule or when another ball is to be played, it should be lifted and dropped as near as possible to the spot where the ball lay, except when a rule permits it to be dropped elsewhere or placed. In a hazard, a lifted ball must be dropped and come to rest in the hazard; if it rolls out of the hazard it must be re-dropped without penalty. On a putting green the ball should be placed.

A ball may only be dropped by the player himself. He stands erect, holds the ball at shoulder height with outstretched arm and drops it. If a ball is dropped in any other way, the player incurs a penalty stroke. If the ball touches the player before it strikes the ground, the player re-drops without penalty. If the ball touches his partner or either of their caddies or equipment before or after it strikes the ground, the ball is re-dropped without penalty.

A ball to be lifted under the rules may be lifted by the player or his partner, or by another person authorised by the

Fig. 15 Lifting the ball

player. It may be lifted for the purpose of identification but must then be replaced on the same spot.

A ball may be cleaned (except when lifted under rules 5–3, 12–2 and 22) when lifted from an unplayable lie, for relief from an obstruction, from casual water, or ground under repair, from a water hazard, on a wrong green, or on the putting green. (*Rules 12–2, 20 and 21*)

Ball interfering with play

Anywhere on the course a player may have any other ball lifted if he considers that it might interfere with his play. A ball so lifted should be replaced after the player has played his stroke. If a ball is accidentally moved when complying with this rule, no penalty is incurred, but the ball so moved should be replaced. (*Rule 22*)

A moving ball

A player may not play while his ball is moving, with the exception of certain cases, e.g. when the ball is moving in water, provided he hits the ball without delay, thus not allowing wind or current to better his position. (*Rule 14–5*)

Ball in motion stopped or deflected

If a ball in motion is accidentally stopped or deflected by any outside agency, it is a 'rub of the green' and the ball is played as it lies, without penalty.

If it accidentally lodges in anything moving, the ball is dropped through the green or in a hazard, or placed on the putting green, as near as possible to the spot where the moving object was when the ball lodged in it, without penalty.

If the player's ball in motion is stopped or deflected by him, his partner or either of their caddies, or their clubs or other equipment, the player or his side is penalised two strokes in stroke play or loses the hole in match play. If two balls in motion collide, each player plays his ball as it lies. (*Rule 19*)

Ball at rest moved

If a ball at rest is moved or the lie is altered by a fellow-competitor, the caddie or any outside agency, the player replaces the ball, without penalty to himself. If it is impossible to determine the exact spot, the ball is dropped (or placed, in the case of the putting green)

as near as possible to the place from which it was moved, and not nearer the hole.

Except while searching for the ball, if it is moved by the opponent in match play the opponent incurs a penalty stroke, and the ball is replaced. If it is moved by the player, whether while searching or not, he incurs a penalty stroke, and the ball is replaced. In stroke play if the ball is moved by a fellow-competitor, there is no penalty but the ball

player or partner

outside agency

Fig. 16 Moving a ball at rest

must be restored to its original position; but if the ball is moved by the player he incurs a penalty stroke. (*Rule 18*)

Ball unfit for play

If a ball in play is so badly damaged that it becomes unfit for further play, it may be changed by the player after agreeing with his opponent or marker that it is so damaged. Mud on a ball does not make it unfit for play. If a ball breaks into pieces as a result of a stroke, it is replaced with another ball without penalty. (*Rule 5–3*)

Ball lost, out of bounds or unplayable

If a ball is lost outside a water hazard or is out of bounds, the player plays his next stroke as nearly as possible at the spot from which the original ball was played or moved by him, adding a penalty stroke to his score for the hole. A ball may be declared unplayable at any place on the course except in a water hazard, and the player is the sole judge as to whether his ball is unplayable.

If a player decides his ball is unplayable he either plays his next stroke as

provided for a ball lost or out of bounds, i.e. the 'stroke and distance' penalty; or drops a ball, under a penalty of one stroke, either within two club-lengths of the point where the ball lay, but not nearer the hole, or behind the point where the ball lay. In this case he must keep that point between himself and the hole, with no limit to how far behind that point the ball may be dropped. If the ball lay in a bunker, a ball must be dropped in the bunker, if relief is taken in this way. (*Rules 27 and 28*)

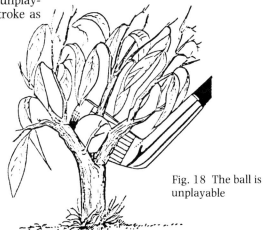

Fig. 18 The ball is unplayable

Fig. 17 Out of bounds

Provisional ball (See *Definitions*)

If a ball might be lost outside a water hazard or may be out of bounds, to save time the player can at once play another ball provisionally, as nearly as possible from the spot at which the original ball was played.

Before playing a provisional ball the player must announce his intention to his opponent or marker, and such a ball may be played only before the player or his partner goes forward to search for the original ball. The player may play a provisional ball until he reaches the place where the original ball is likely to be.

If he plays any strokes with the provisional ball from the point beyond that place, the original ball is deemed to be lost, even if it is later found. If the original ball is lost outside a water hazard or is out of bounds, he continues play with the provisional ball, under penalty of stroke and distance. If the original ball is unplayable in bounds, or lies or is lost in a water hazard, the provisional ball is adandoned. (*Rule 27–2*)

Obstructions (See *Definitions*)

Any movable obstruction may be removed before a shot is played. If the obstruction is immovable, or the ball lies on or touches the movable obstruction, the ball may be lifted and dropped not more than one club-length away from the point where relief is obtained; such point is determined as the nearest point to where the ball lay. The ball is dropped, without penalty, and must come to rest not nearer the hole. (*Rule 24*)

Casual water

If a player's ball lies in or touches casual water, ground under repair or a hole, cast or runway made by a burrowing animal, reptile or bird; or if any of these conditions interfere with the player's stance or the area of his intended swing, he may drop a ball (without penalty) on ground which avoids these conditions. It must be within one club-length of the point where the player gets relief, and such point shall be determined as the nearest point to where the ball lay. He

Fig. 20 Casual water: ball may be ▶ moved from 1 to 2

may also drop a ball similarly in a hazard without penalty; if a ball is dropped clear of the hazard there is a penalty stroke.

If a ball lies on the putting green and in casual water, or if casual water intervenes between it and the hole, the ball may be lifted and placed, without penalty, on the nearest spot (not nearer the hole) which will give a clear line to the hole. (*Rule 25*)

Fig. 19 Immovable obstruction: ball may be dropped within one club length (C) of the nearest point of relief (B)

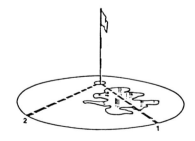

Hazards and water hazards

(See *Definitions*)

When the ball lies in or touches a hazard or water hazard, nothing may be done which can in any way improve its lie. Before making a stroke, the player cannot touch the ground or water with his club, nor touch or move any loose impediment in the hazard.

If the ball lies or is lost in a water hazard, the player can play the ball as it lies, or, under a penalty of one stroke, drop a ball: behind the water hazard, without limit as to distance, keeping the spot at which the ball last crossed the margin of the hazard between himself and the hole; or as near as possible to the spot from which the original ball was played.

A player may drop a ball outside a lateral water hazard within two club-lengths of the margin of either side, opposite the point where the ball last crossed the hazard margin. The ball must come to rest not nearer the hole than this point.

Note Hazards are of various kinds, but bunkers form by far the greatest number of such hazards on most golf courses. Bunkers are depressions in the ground filled with sand, and usually built up on the side nearest the hole so that the player must loft the ball out, thus losing considerable distance in relation to an opponent lying on the fairway. Most bunkers, however, are around the greens, and considerable skill is required to get the ball out and near enough to the hole to have a chance of getting down in one putt. (*Rule 13–4 and 26*)

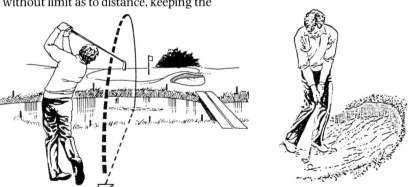

Fig. 21 Water hazard

Fig. 22 Touching the ground with the club before the stroke is prohibited

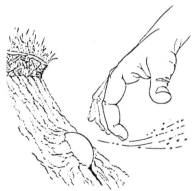

Fig. 23 Scraping sand to see top of ball

The flagstick

Before or during the stroke, the player may have the flagstick removed or held up at any time to indicate the position of the hole. This may be done only on the authority of the player before he plays his stroke. If the flagstick is attended or removed by an opponent, a fellow competitor or the caddie of either, with the knowledge of the player, and no objection is made, the player is deemed to have authorised it.

If a player's ball strikes the flagstick when it is attended or has been removed, strikes the person standing at the flagstick or equipment carried by him, or strikes an unattended flagstick when played from the putting green, the player incurs a penalty of loss of hole in match play, or two strokes in stroke play.

If the ball is played from off the green and comes to rest against the flagstick when it is in the hole, the player is entitled to have the flagstick removed, and if the ball falls into the hole the player is deemed to have holed out at his last stroke. (*Rule 17*)

Fig. 25 The flagstick ▶

◀ Fig. 24 Flagstick being held to indicate position of hole

The putting green

The line of the putt must not be touched except as provided in the rules, but the player may place the club in front of the ball when addressing it, without pressing anything down. The player may move any loose impediment on the putting green by picking it up or brushing it aside with his hand or a club, without pressing anything down. If the ball is moved, it is replaced without penalty.

The player may repair damage to the putting green caused by the impact of a ball and old hole plugs. The ball may be marked and lifted to permit repair and then replaced on the spot from which it was lifted.

A ball lying on the putting green may be marked and lifted without penalty, cleaned if desired, and replaced on the spot from which it was lifted.

When the ball nearer the hole lies on the putting green, if the player considers it might interfere with his play, he may require the opponent to mark and lift the ball, which must be replaced after the player has played his stroke.

Anyone on the player's side may, before a stroke is made, point out a line for putting, but the following are prohibited: placing a mark on the green;

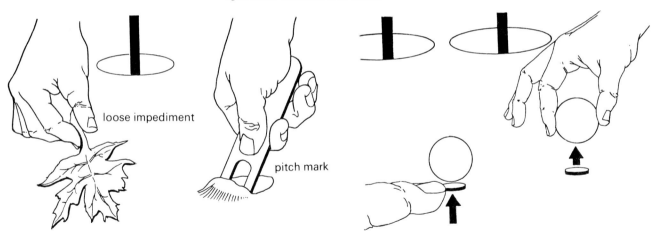

Fig. 26 On the putting green

Fig. 27 Lifting the ball is allowed

touching the line of the putt in front of, to the side of, or behind the hole; testing the surface of the green, rolling a ball on it or roughening or scraping the surface; playing before the other ball is at rest; standing so as to influence the position or movement of the ball; lifting the other ball while the player's ball is in motion.

A ball lying on a putting green other than that of the hole being played must be lifted and dropped off the putting green, not nearer the hole, as near as possible to where the ball lay. There is no penalty.

The player may not make a stroke on the putting green from a stance astride, or with either foot touching, the line of the putt or an extension of the line behind the ball.

If a player putts out of turn during match play, the opponent may require the stroke to be replayed. A ball moved by another ball must be replaced.

In match play a player after holing out may remove his opponent's ball provided it is at rest, and claim the hole or concede the half as the case may be. If the opponent's ball is not removed and it falls into the hole (before the time limit

expires) the opponent is deemed to have holed out at his last stroke.

In stroke play, if the ball nearer the hole is in the way of or affecting the playing of the other ball in any way, it may be played first or marked and lifted while the other ball is played, but only at the request of the player about to putt.

In stroke play the ball may be lifted or putted first if the owner considers it might be of assistance to a fellow competitor.

When both balls lie on the putting green, if the competitor's ball strikes the other he incurs a penalty of two strokes and plays the ball as it lies. The other ball is replaced at once. (*Rules 16 and 19*)

Fig. 28 Touching the line of putt in front of, to the side of or behind the hole is prohibited

The hole

The 'hole' must be $4\frac{1}{4}$ inches (108 mm) in diameter and at least 4 inches (100 mm) deep. If a lining is used it should be sunk at least 1 inch (25 mm) below the putting green surface, unless the nature of the soil makes it impractical to do so. Its outer diameter should not exceed $4\frac{1}{4}$ inches (108 mm). (See *Definitions*)

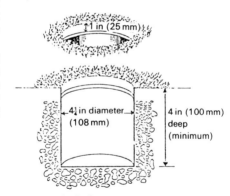

Fig. 29 The hole

Readers are strongly advised to read the Rules of Golf in full, but for their information Sections I and II concerning Etiquette and Definitions are reproduced here.

Etiquette

Courtesy on the course

Safety

Prior to playing a stroke or making a practice swing, the player should ensure that no one is standing close by or in a position to be hit by the club, the ball or any stones, pebbles, twigs or the like which may be moved by the stroke or swing.

Consideration for other players

The player who has the honour should be allowed to play before his opponent or fellow-competitor tees his ball.

No one should move, talk or stand close to or directly behind the ball or the hole when a player is addressing the ball or making a stroke.

In the interest of all, players should play without delay.

No player should play until the players in front are out of range.

Players searching for a ball should signal the players behind them to pass as soon as it becomes apparent that the ball will not easily be found. They should not search for five minutes before doing so. They should not continue play until the players following them have passed and are out of range.

When the play of a hole has been completed, players should immediately leave the putting green.

Priority on the course

In the absence of special rules, two-ball matches should have precedence over and be entitled to pass any three- or four-ball match.

A single player has no standing and should give way to a match of any kind.

Any match playing a whole round is entitled to pass a match playing a shorter round.

If a match fails to keep its place on the course and loses more than one clear hole on the players in front, it should invite the match following to pass.

Care of the course

Holes in bunkers

Before leaving a bunker, a player should carefully fill up and smooth over all holes and footprints made by him.

Replace divots; repair ball-marks and damage by spikes

Through the green, a player should ensure that any turf cut or displaced by him is replaced at once and pressed down and that any damage to the putting green made by a ball is carefully repaired. Damage to the putting green caused by golf shoe spikes should be repaired *on completion of the hole.*

Damage to greens – flagsticks, bags, etc.

Players should ensure that, when putting down bags or the flagstick, no damage is done to the putting green and that neither they nor their caddies damage the hole by standing close to it, in handling the flagstick or in removing the ball from the hole. The flagstick should be properly replaced in the hole before the players leave the putting green. Players should not damage the putting green by leaning on their putters, particularly when removing the ball from the hole.

Golf carts

Local notices regulating the movement of golf carts should be strictly observed.

Damage through practice swings

In taking practice swings, players should avoid causing damage to the course, particularly the tees, by removing divots.

Definitions

Addressing the ball

A player has 'addressed the ball' when he has taken his stance and has also grounded his club, except that in a hazard a player has addressed the ball when he has taken his stance.

Advice

'Advice' is any counsel or suggestion which could influence a player in determining his play, the choice of a club, or the method of making a stroke.

Information on the Rules or Local Rules, or on matters of public information such as the position of hazards or the flagstick on the putting green, is not advice.

Ball deemed to move

A ball is deemed to have 'moved' if it leaves its position and comes to rest in any other place.

When the ball comes to rest, it is ▶
deemed to have 'moved'

Ball in play, provisional ball, wrong ball

a A ball is 'in play' as soon as the player has made a stroke on the teeing ground. It remains as his ball in play until holed out, except when it is out of bounds, lost or lifted, or another ball has been substituted under applicable Rule or Local Rule: a ball so substituted becomes the ball in play.

b A 'provisional ball' is a ball played under Rule 27–2 for a ball which may be lost outside a water hazard or may be out of bounds. It ceases to be a provisional ball when the Rule provides either that the player continues play with it as the ball in play or that it be abandoned.

c A 'wrong ball' is any ball other than the ball in play or a provisional ball or, in stroke play, a second ball in accordance with Rule 3–3 or 20–7b.

Ball lost

A ball is 'lost' if:

a it is not found, or is not identified as his by the player, within five minutes after the player's side or his or their caddies have begun to search for it; or

b the player has put another ball into play under the Rules, even though he may not have searched for the original ball; or

c the player has played any stroke with a provisional ball from a point nearer the hole than the place where the original ball is likely to be, whereupon the provisional ball becomes the ball in play.

Time spent in playing a wrong ball is not counted in the five-minute period allowed for search.

The ball is in play once the player ▶
has made a stroke

Caddie

A 'caddie' is one who carries or handles a player's clubs during play and otherwise assists him in accordance with the Rules.

Committee

The 'Committee' is the committee in charge of the competition, or, if the matter does not arise in a competition, the committee in charge of the course.

When one caddie is employed by more than one player, he is always deemed to be the caddie of the player whose ball is involved, and equipment carried by him is deemed to be that player's equipment, except when the caddie acts upon specific directions from another player, in which case he is considered to be that other player's caddie.

Casual water

'Casual water' is any temporary accumulation of water which is visible before or after the player takes his stance and which is not in a water hazard. Snow and ice are either casual water or loose impediments, at the option of the player. Dew is not casual water.

Competitor

A 'competitor' is a player in a stroke competition. A 'fellow competitor' is any person with whom the competitor plays. Neither is partner of the other. In stroke play foursome and four-ball competitions, where the context so admits, the word 'competitor' or 'fellow competitor' shall be held to include his partner.

Course

The 'course' is the whole area within which play is permitted. (*Rule 33–2*)

Equipment

'Equipment' is anything used, worn or carried by or for the player except any ball he has played and any small object, such as a coin or a tee, when used to mark the position of a ball or the extent of an area in which a ball is to be dropped. Equipment includes a golf cart, whether or not motorised. If such a cart is shared by more than one player, its status under the Rules is the same as that of a caddie employed by more than one player. See 'Caddie'.

Flagstick

The 'flagstick' is a movable straight indicator provided by the Committee, with or without bunting or other material attached, centred in the hole to show its position. It shall be circular in cross-section.

Forecaddie

A 'forecaddie' is one who is employed by the Committee to indicate to players the position of balls on the course, and is an 'outside agency'.

Ground under repair

'Ground under repair' is any portion of the course so marked by order of the committee concerned or so declared by its authorised representative. It includes material piled for removal and a hole made by a greenkeeper, even if not so marked. Stakes and lines defining ground under repair are in such ground.

Note 1 Grass cuttings and other material left on the course which have been abandoned and are not intended to be removed are not ground under repair unless so marked.

Note 2 The Committee may make a Local Rule prohibiting play from ground under repair.

Hazards

A 'hazard' is any bunker or water hazard.

Hole

The 'hole' shall be $4\frac{1}{4}$ inches (108 mm) in diameter and at least 4 inches (100 mm) deep. If a lining is used, it shall be sunk at least 1 inch (25 mm) below the putting green surface unless the nature of the soil makes it impracticable to do so; its outer diameter shall not exceed $4\frac{1}{4}$ (108 mm).

Holed

A ball is 'holed' when it lies within the circumference of the hole and all of it is below the level of the lip of the hole.

Honour

The side which is entitled to play first from the teeing grounds is said to have the 'honour'.

Lateral water hazard

A 'lateral water hazard' is a water hazard or that part of a water hazard so situated that it is not possible, or is deemed by the Committee to be impracticable, to drop a ball behind the water hazard and keep the spot at which the ball last crossed the hazard margin between the player and the hole. That part of the water hazard to be played as a lateral water hazard should be distinctively marked.

Note Lateral water hazards should be defined by red stakes or lines.

Loose impediments

The term 'loose impediments' denotes natural objects not fixed or growing and not adhering to the ball, and includes stones not solidly embedded, leaves, twigs, branches, and the like, dung worms and insects and casts or heaps made by them. Snow and ice are either casual water or loose impediments, at the option of the player.

Sand and loose soil are loose impediments on the putting green, but not elsewhere on the course.

Playing out of a hazard ▶

Lost ball —*See* Ball lost

Marker

A 'marker' is a scorer in stroke play who is appointed by the Committee to record a competitor's score. He may be a fellow competitor. He is not a referee. A marker should not lift a ball or mark its position unless authorised to do so by the competitor and, unless he is a fellow competitor, should not attend the flagstick or stand at the hole or mark its position.

29

Matches —*See* **Sides and Matches**

Observer

An 'observer' is appointed by the Committee to assist a referee to decide questions of fact and to report to him any breach of a Rule or Local Rule. An observer should not attend the flagstick, stand at or mark the position of the hole, or lift the ball or mark its position.

Obstructions

An 'obstruction' is anything artificial, whether erected, placed or left on the course, including artificial surfaces of roads and paths, but excepting:
a objects defining out of bounds, such as walls, fences, stakes and railings
b any part of an immovable artificial object which is out of bounds
c any construction declared by the Committee to be an integral part of the course.

Out of bounds

'Out of bounds' is ground on which play is prohibited.

When out of bounds is defined by reference to stakes or a fence, the out of bounds line is determined by the nearest inside points of the stakes or fence posts at ground level excluding angled supports. When out of bounds is fixed by a line on the grounds the line itself is out of bounds.

A ball is out of bounds when all of it lies out of bounds.

The out of bounds line is deemed to extend vertically upwards and downwards.

The player may stand out of bounds to play a ball lying within bounds.

Outside agency

An 'outside agency' is any agency not part of the match or, in stroke play, not part of a competitor's side, and includes a referee, a marker, an observer, or a forecaddie.

Neither wind nor water is an outside agency.

Partner

A 'partner' is a player associated with another player on the same side. In a threesome, foursome, or a four-ball

where the context so admits, the word 'player' shall be held to include his partner.

Penalty stroke

A 'penalty stroke' is one added to the score of a side under certain Rules. In a threesome or foursome, penalty strokes do not affect the order of play.

Provisional ball

A 'provisional ball' is a ball played under Rule 27–2 for a ball which may be lost outside a water hazard or may be out of bounds. It ceases to be a provisional ball when the Rule provides either that the player continue play with it as the ball in play or that it be abandoned.

Putting green

The 'putting green' is all ground of the hole being played which is specially prepared for putting or otherwise defined as such by the Committee.

A ball is deemed to be on the putting green when any part of it touches the putting green.

Referee

A 'referee' is one who is appointed by the Committee to accompany the players to decide questions of fact and apply the Rules of Golf. He shall act on any breach of Rule or Local Rule which he may observe or which may be reported to him.

A referee should not attend the flagstick, stand at or mark the position of the hole or lift the ball or mark its position.

Rub of the green

A 'rub of the green' occurs when a ball in motion is stopped or deflected by any outside agency. (*Rule 19–1*)

Sides and matches

Side: a player or two or more players who are partners.
Single: a match in which one plays against another.
Threesome: a match in which one plays against two, and each side plays one ball.
Foursome: a match in which two play against two, and each side plays one ball.
Three-ball: a match in which three play against one another, each playing his own ball.
Best-ball: a match in which one plays against the better ball of two or the best ball of three players.
Four-ball: a match in which two play their better ball against the better ball of two other players.

Note In a best-ball or four-ball match, if a partner is absent for reasons satisfactory to the Committee, the remaining member(s) of his side may represent the side.

Stance

Taking the 'stance' consists in a player placing his feet in position for and preparatory to making a stroke.

On the putting green ▶

Stipulated round

The 'stipulated round' consists of playing the holes of the course in their correct sequence unless otherwise authorised by the Committee. The number of holes in a stipulated round is 18 unless a smaller number is authorised by the Committee.

In match play, only, the Committee may, for the purpose of settling a tie, extend the stipulated round to as many holes as are required for a match to be won. (*Rule 2–4*)

Stroke

A 'stroke' is the forward movement of the club made with the intention of fairly striking at and moving the ball. If a player checks his downswing voluntarily before the club-head reaches the ball, he is deemed not to have made a stroke.

Teeing ground

The 'teeing ground' is the starting place for the hole to be played. It is a rectangular area two club-lengths in depth, the front and the sides of which are defined by the outside limits of two tee markers.

A ball is outside the teeing ground when all of it lies outside the stipulated area. When playing the first stroke with any ball (including a provisional ball) from the teeing ground, the tee markers are immovable obstructions.

Through the green

'Through the green' is the whole area of the course except:
a teeing ground and putting green of the hole being played
b all hazards on the course.

Water hazard

A 'water hazard' is any sea, lake, pond, river, ditch, surface drainage ditch or other open water course (whether or not containing water) and anything of a similar nature.

All ground or water within the margin of a water hazard is part of the water hazard. The margin of a water hazard is deemed to extend vertically upwards. Stakes and lines defining the margins of water hazards are in the hazard.

Note Water hazards (other than lateral water hazards) should be defined by yellow stakes or lines.

Wrong ball

A 'wrong ball' is any ball other than:
a the ball in play
b a provisional ball or
c in stroke play, a second ball played under Rule 3–3 or Rule 20–7b
d a ball substituted under an applicable Rule which does not permit substitution.

Making a stroke ▶